SCHIRMER'S LIBRARY OF MUSICAL CLASSICS

OTAKAR ŠEVČIK

Op. 7

Preparatory Trill Studies

(Estudios Preparatorios de Trino)

For the Violin

For Developing the Touch and Strength
and Surety of the Fingers

Edited by
LOUIS SVEĆENSKI

IN TWO PARTS

→ PART I
Exercises in the First Position
Library Vol. 1413

PART II
Exercises in the Second, Third, Fourth,
Fifth and Sixth Positions
Library Vol. 1414

G. SCHIRMER, Inc.

DISTRIBUTED BY
HAL•LEONARD®
CORPORATION
7777 W. BLUEMOUND RD. P.O. BOX 13819 MILWAUKEE, WI 53213

AL DISCÍPULO

La práctica del trino debe incluírse en la obra técnica del diario por el discípulo del violín, no sólamente por el trino, sino para el desarrollo de un movimiento exacto y seguro de los dedos en general.

La dificultad en obtener un trino claro y resonante en la mayor parte de los casos se aumenta por una defectuosa posición de la mano y los dedos que puede corregirse si el discípulo observa fielmente las siguientes instrucciones.

Antes de empezar a tocar el ejercicio deben colocarse los dedos sobre los tonos indicados por las notas negras sin plica, y después de haber asegurado su verdadera entonación, los dedos deben mantenerse sobre las cuerdas por lo menos un minuto, siendo esencial que el discípulo, durante este intervalo, *fije los ojos sobre la mano y los dedos.* Al empezar el ejercicio los dedos deben alejarse de las cuerdas *sin cambiar la posición en que estaban cuando sobre los tonos indicados.*

Practíquese el trino despaciosamente con cuidadosa atención a la uniformidad del movimiento de los dedos y ensáyese la calidad y claridad del trino en *piano* y aún en *pianíssimo.*

Es de suma importancia retener los dedos en su lugar según se indica por la línea amparando la obra de los dedos, y el discípulo debe tener muy presente que únicamente siguiendo estas indicaciones podrá derivar beneficio completo de estos ejercicios.

Anotación.—Estos ejercicios preparatorios de trino deben darse al discípulo encuanto este listo para empezar el estudio del primer libro de Kayser, Op. 20.

Louis Svećenski.

30092-109

TO THE STUDENT

The practice of the trill should be included in the daily technical work of the Violin Student, not only for the trill itself, but also for promoting the development of accurate and reliable finger-action in general.

The difficulty in obtaining a clear and ringing trill is increased, in most cases, by a faulty position of the hand and fingers, which may be corrected if the student will faithfully observe the following instructions.

Before beginning to play the exercise the fingers should be placed on the tones indicated by black noteheads, and, after having made sure of their true intonation, the fingers should be kept on the strings for at least one minute, during which time *the student's eyes should be fixed upon his hand and fingers.* When ready to start the exercise, the fingers should leave the strings *without changing the position in which they were kept while on the tones indicated.*

Practise the trill slowly, with close attention to the evenness of the finger-movement, and test the tone-quality and clarity of the trill in *piano* and even *pianissimo.*

To retain the fingers in their places as indicated by the line following the fingerwork is of the greatest importance, and the student should be convinced that only by following these instructions can full benefit be derived from these exercises.

Note.—These preparatory Trill Exercises should be given to students as soon as they are ready to begin the study of the first book of Kayser's Op. 20.

Louis Svećenski.

AVIS A L'ÉLÈVE

*L'*élève consacrera une partie du temps à l'étude du trille dans le travail journalier de la technique du violon et cela non seulement pour le trille en lui-même, mais aussi pour la dextérité des doigts en général.

En beaucoup de cas la difficulté pour obtenir un trille sonnant clairement est augmentée par la mauvaise position de la main et des doigts; pour réduire cette difficulté au minimum l'élève observera avec soin les instructions suivantes.

Avant de commencer à jouer l'exercice, les doigts devront être placés sur les sons indiqués par les notes noires, et après s'être assuré de la parfaite justesse, l'élève gardera les doigts sur les cordes au moins une minute *durant laquelle il aura les yeux fixés sur la main et les doigts.* Commençant l'exercice, les doigts devront se lever des cordes *sans changer la position dans laquelle ils étaient tenus quand ils étaient placés sur les sons indiqués.*

Il faut travailler lentement avec l'attention fixée sur l'égalité des mouvements du doigt et il faut cultiver la clarté et la qualité de son du trille dans les nuances *piano* et *pianissimo.*

La tenue correcte des doigts étant d'une très grande importance, l'élève devra se convaincre que ce sera seulement en suivant ces instructions à la lettre qu'il parviendra à en tirer tout le bénéfice possible.

Nota.—Ces exercices préparatoires pour le trille devront être travaillés par les élèves aussitôt qu'ils seront prêts à commencer l'étude du premier livre de Kayser, Op. 20.

Louis Svećenski.

Estudios Preparatorios de Trino
En la primera posición
Parte Iᵃ

Preparatory Trill Studies
In the first position
Part I

Exercices Préparatoires de Trille
Dans la 1ʳᵉ position
Partie Iʳᵉ

Edited by Louis Svećenski

Otakar Ševčík. Op. 7

1

Semitono: 1-2 dedo

Practíquese este ejercicio en las seis siguientes maneras.

Semitone: fingers 1-2

Practise this exercise in the following six manners:

Demi-ton: 1-2 doigt

On travaillera cet exercice des six manières suivantes:

Colóquense los dedos sobre las tres notas negras antes de empezar este ejercicio.
Place fingers on the three black notes before beginning this exercise.
Placez les doigts sur les trois notes noires avant de commencer cet exercice.

*Levántese bien el dedo, dejándolo caer sobre la cuerda con fuerza y absoluta seguridad.

**Mauténgause les dedos sobre las cuerdas.

*Lift the finger well and let it fall upon the string with force and absolute precision.

**The fingers to be kept on the strings to end of lines.

*Bien lever le doigt et le laisser tomber sur la corde avec force et avec précision.

**Laissez les doigts en place.

Printed in the U. S. A.

2

Semitono: **2-3 dedo** | Semitone: fingers **2-3** | Demi-ton: **2-3 doigt**

* Mauténgause los dedos sobre las cuerdas (véase N° 1). | * The fingers to be kept on the strings (see No. 1). | * Laissez les doigts en place (voir N° 1).

6

3

Semitonos: **0-1.,3-4** dedo | Semitones: fingers **0-1, 3-4** | Demi-tons: **0-1,3-4** doigt

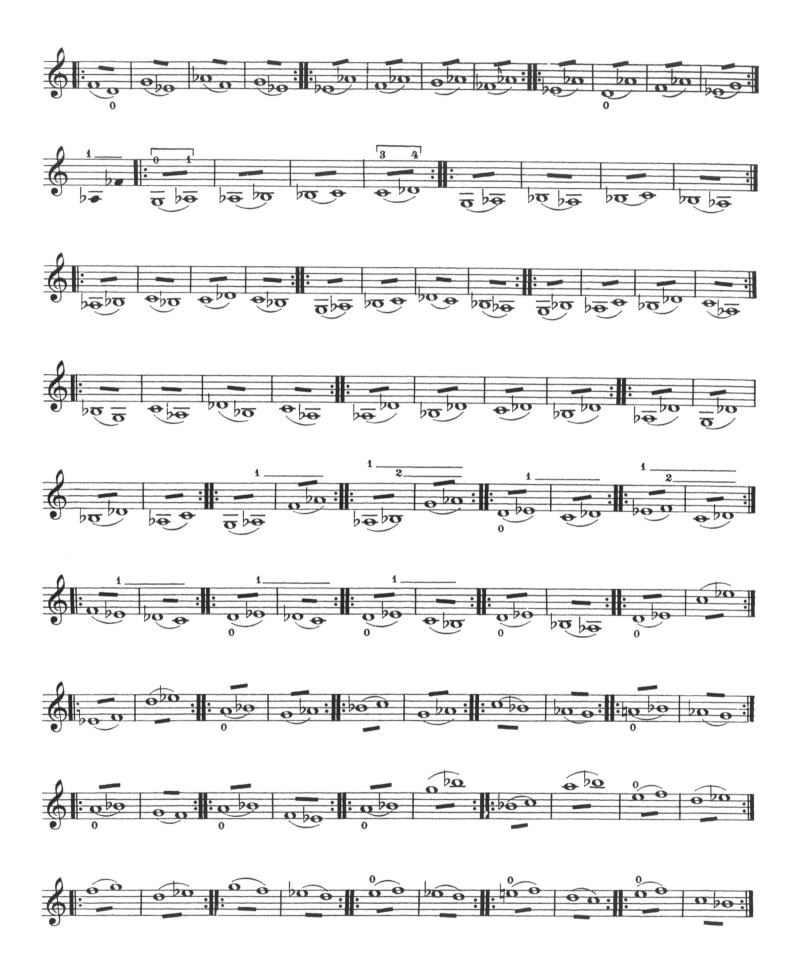

4

Accidentales	Accidentals	Signes accidentels
Pasajes cromáticos	Chromatic passages	Gamme chromatique

5

Escalas | Scales | Gammes

12

Mi mayor _ E major _ Mi majeur

Mi menor _ E minor _ Mi mineur

La menor _ A minor _ La mineur

Fa mayor _ F major _ Fa majeur

Re menor _ D minor _ Ré mineur

30092

Sib mayor _ Bb major _ Sib majeur

Sol menor _ G minor _ Sol mineur

Mib mayor _ Eb major _ Mib majeur

Do menor _ C minor _ Ut mineur

Lab mayor _ Ab major _ Lab majeur

14

Fa menor — F minor — Fa mineur

Re♭ mayor — D♭ major — Ré♭ majeur

Si♭ menor — B♭ minor — Si♭ mineur

Sol♭ mayor — G♭ major — Sol♭ majeur

Mi♭ menor — E♭ minor — Mi♭ mineur

30092

Si mayor — B major — Si majeur

Si menor — B minor — Si mineur

Fa♯ menor — F♯ minor — Fa♯ mineur

Do♯ menor — C♯ minor — Do♯ mineur

Sol♯ menor — G♯ minor — Sol♯ mineur

6

Triadas Mayores | Major triads | Triades majeures

Mi mayor — E major — Mi majeur

La mayor — A major — La majeur

Re mayor — D major — Ré majeur

Sol mayor _ G major _ Sol majeur

Do mayor _ C major _ Ut majeur

Fa mayor _ F major _ Fa majeur

Si♭ mayor _ B♭ major _ Si♭ majeur

Mi♭ mayor _ E♭ major _ Mi♭ majeur

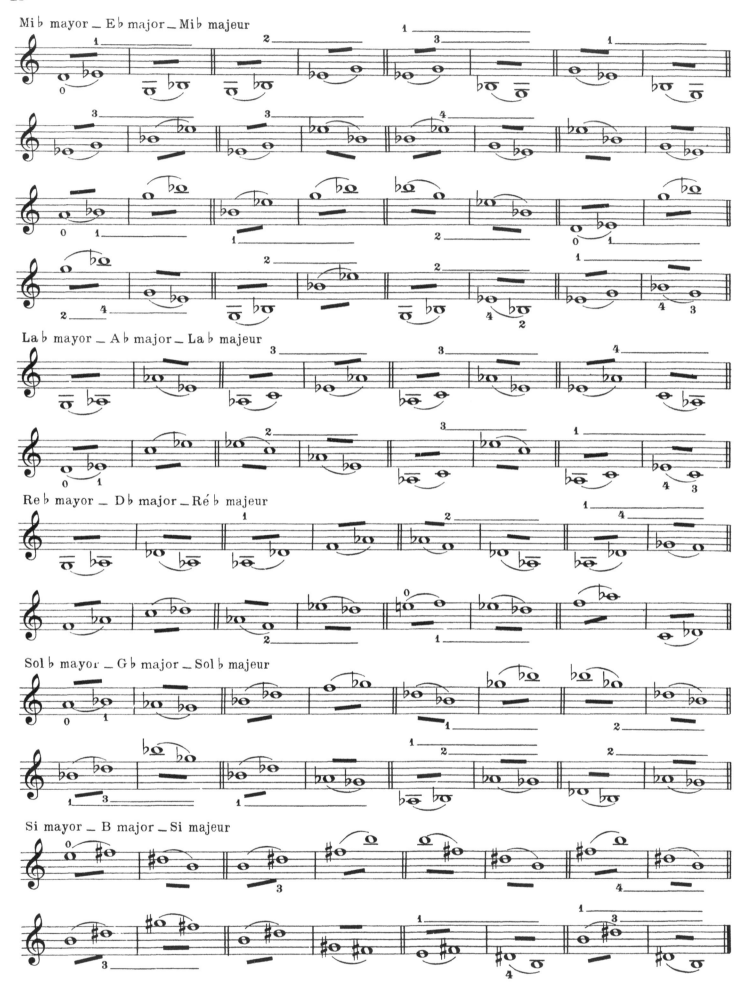

La♭ mayor _ A♭ major _ La♭ majeur

Re♭ mayor _ D♭ major _ Ré♭ majeur

Sol♭ mayor _ G♭ major _ Sol♭ majeur

Si mayor _ B major _ Si majeur

7

Triadas Menores	Minor Triads	Triades mineures
La quinta aumentada y la cuarta disminuida.	The augmented fifth and diminished fourth.	La quinte augmentée et la quarte diminuée.

Si menor _ B minor _ Si mineur

Mi menor _ E minor _ Mi mineur

La menor _ A minor _ La mineur

Re menor _ D minor _ Ré mineur

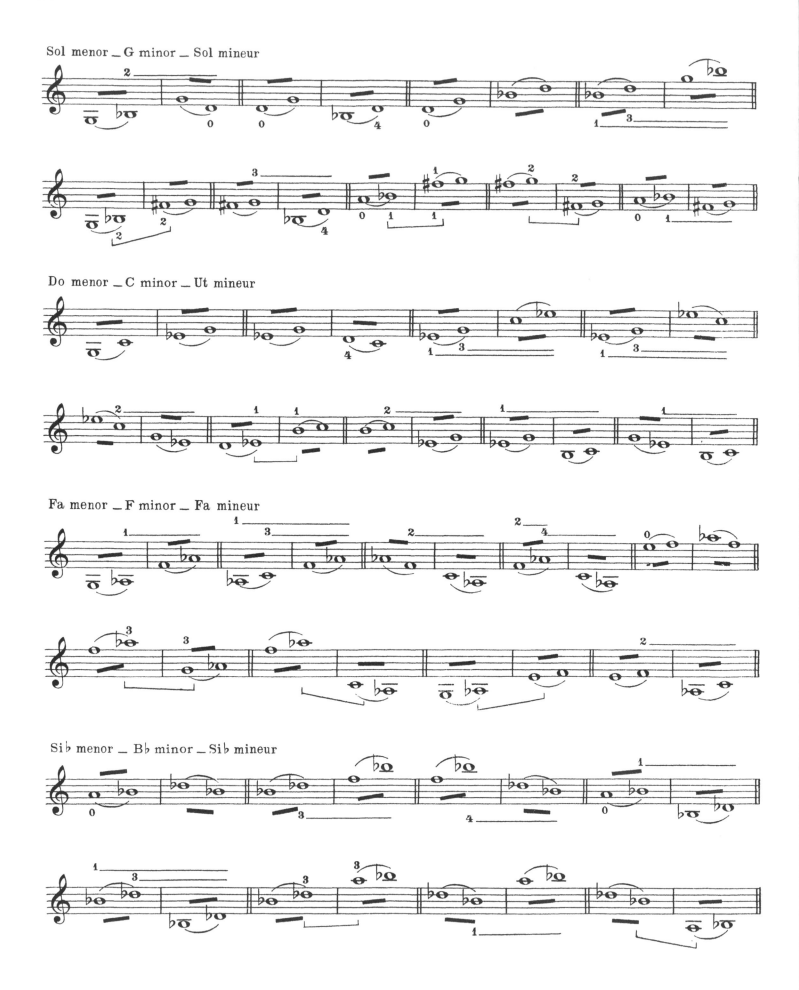

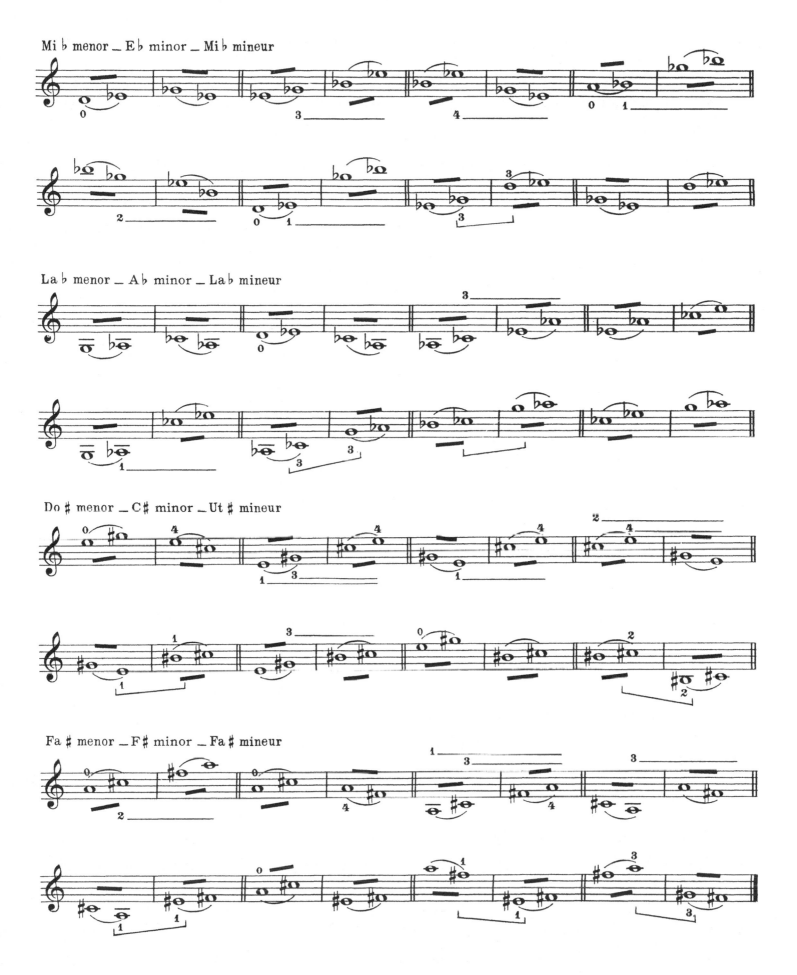

Mi♭ menor — E♭ minor — Mi♭ mineur

La♭ menor — A♭ minor — La♭ mineur

Do♯ menor — C♯ minor — Ut♯ mineur

Fa♯ menor — F♯ minor — Fa♯ mineur

8

La Triada
en todas las claves mayores y menores.

The Triad
in all major and minor keys.

La Triade
dans tous les tons majeurs et mineurs.

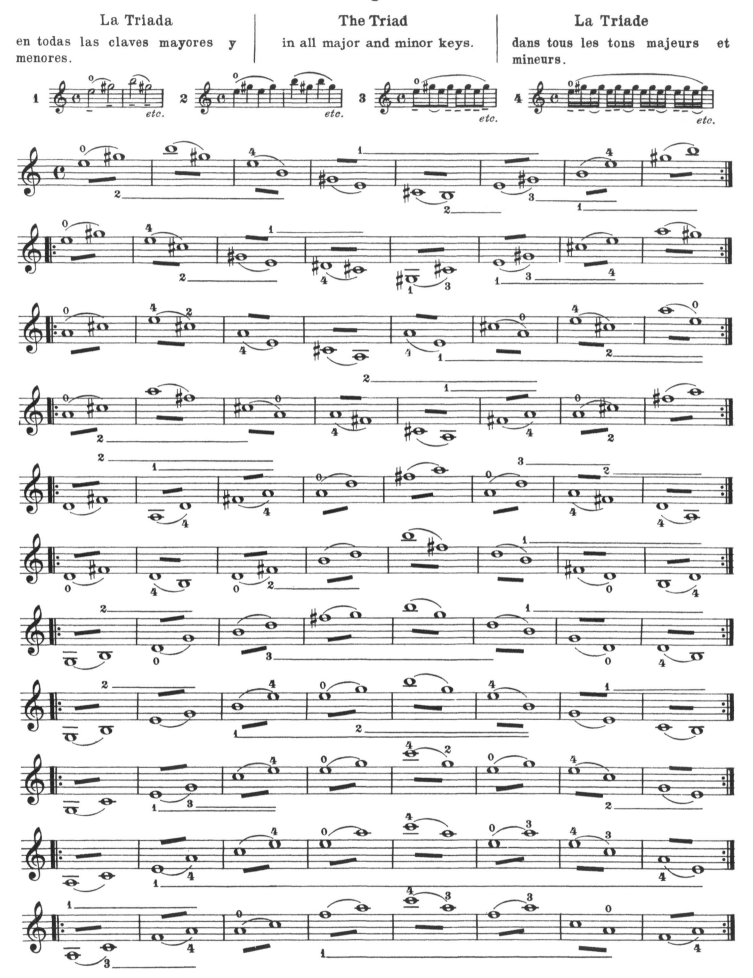

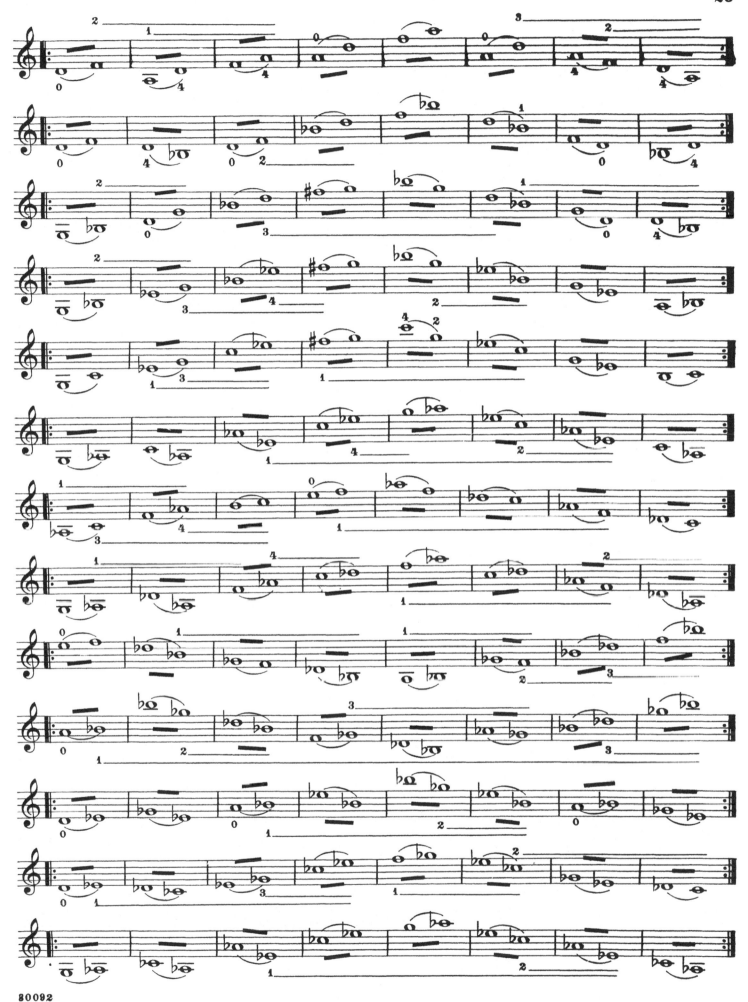

9

Escalas Menores Armónicas	Harmonic minor scales	Gammes mineures harmoniques
La segunda aumentata	The augmented second	La seconde augmentée

Mi menor _ E minor _ Mi mineur

La menor _ A minor _ La mineur

Re menor _ D minor _ Ré mineur

Sol menor _ G minor _ Sol mineur

Do menor _ C minor _ Ut mineur

Fa menor _ F minor _ Fa mineur

Si ♭ menor _ B♭ minor _ Si ♭ mineur

Mi ♭ menor _ E♭ minor _ Mi ♭ mineur

La ♭ menor _ A♭ minor _ La ♭ mineur

Sol ♯ menor _ G♯ minor _ Sol ♯ mineur

Do ♯ menor _ C♯ minor _ Ut ♯ mineur

Fa ♯ menor _ F♯ minor _ Fa ♯ mineur

Si menor _ B minor _ Si mineur

10

Acorde de Séptima del 5º grado	Chord of the Seventh on the 5th degree	Accord de Septième du 5me degré
La Quinta disminuida y la Cuarta aumentada.	The diminished fifth and the augmented fourth.	La quinte diminuée et la quarte augmentée.

11

Extensión del 4º dedo | Extension of the fourth finger | Extension 1u 4º doigt

12

Trinos sin terminación | Trills without after-beat | Trille sans terminaison

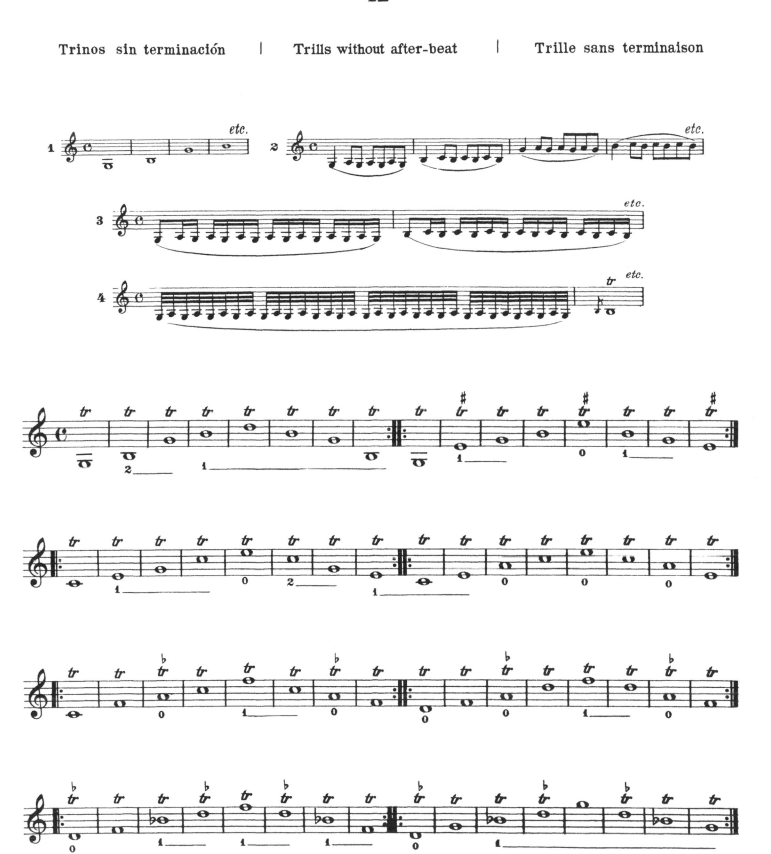

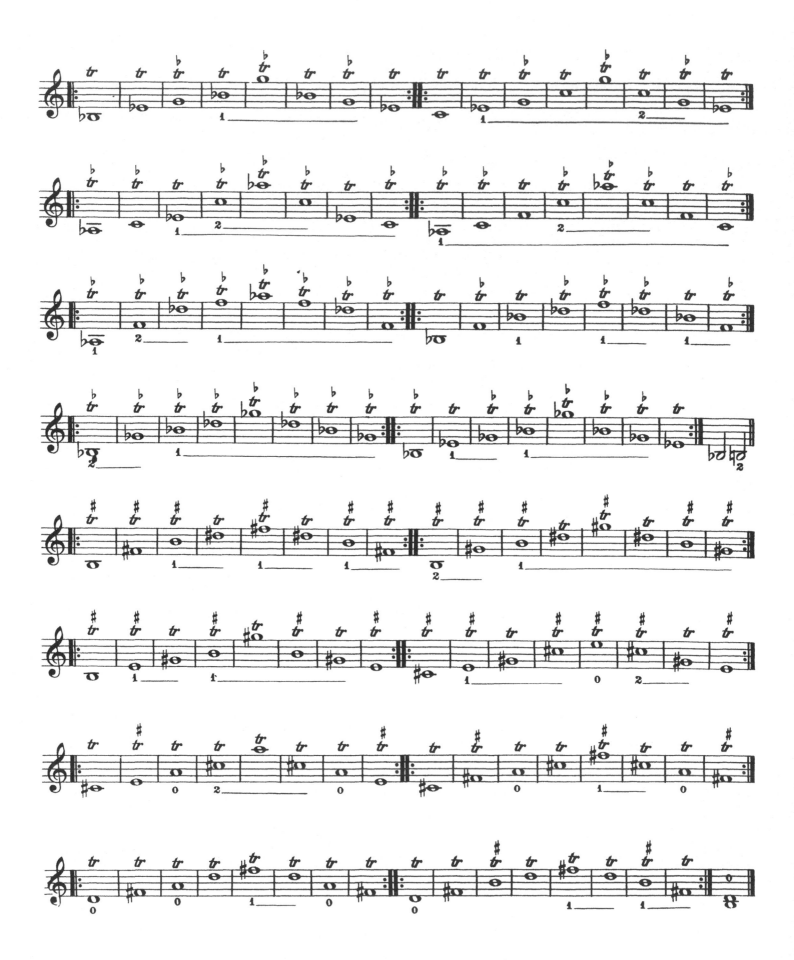

13

14

Trinos con terminación | Trills with after-beat | Trille avec terminaison

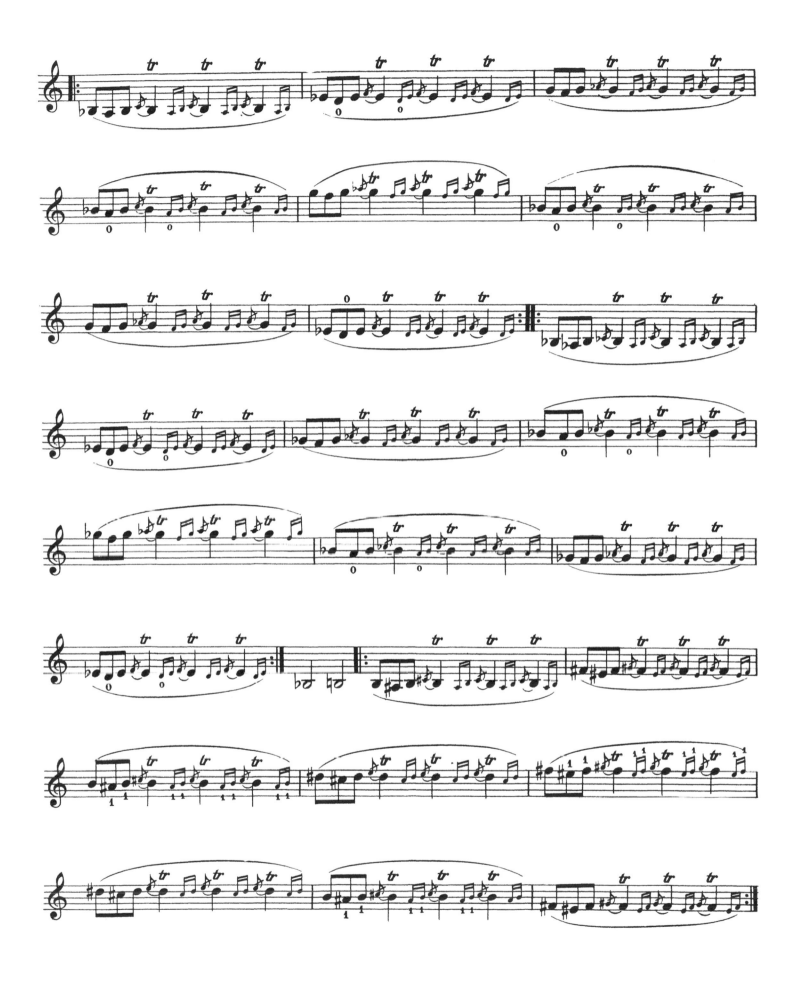

15

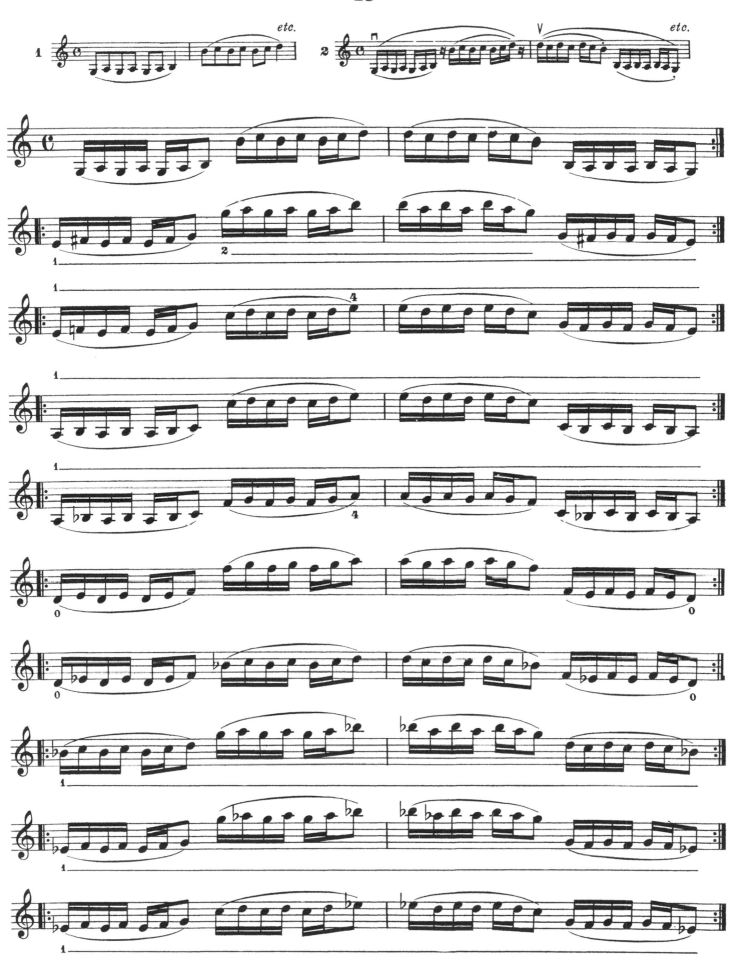

16

17

18

19

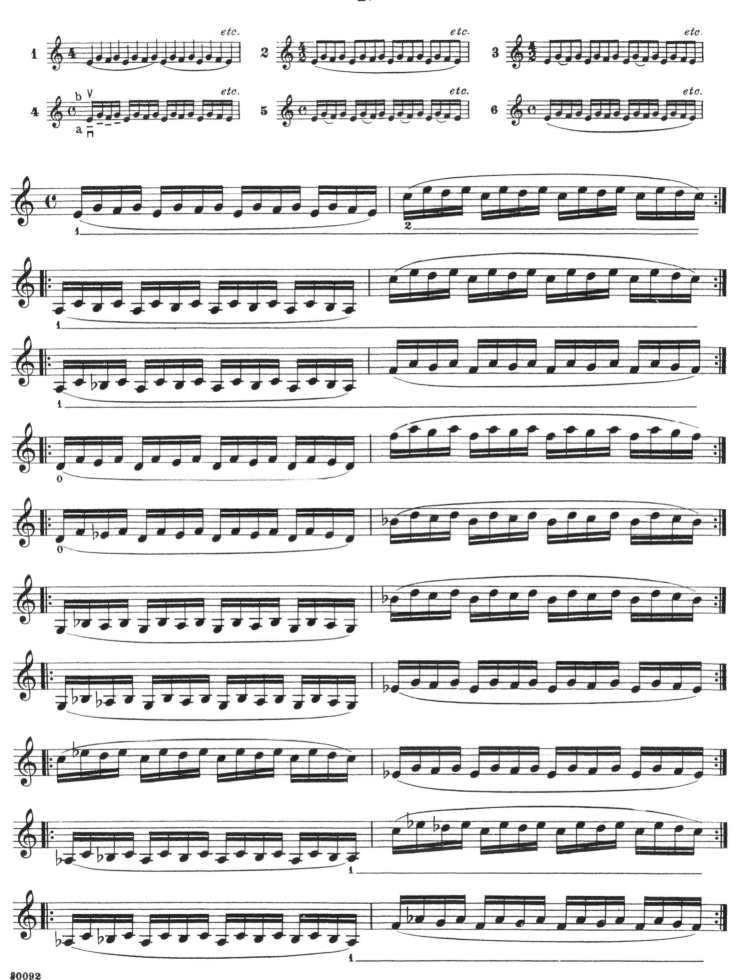

20

Ejercicios en Notas Dobles	Exercises in double notes	Exercice en doubles notes
Triadas	Triads	Triades

21

Acorde de Séptima
del 5º grado

Chord of the Seventh
on the 5th degree

Accord de Septième
du 5me degré

22

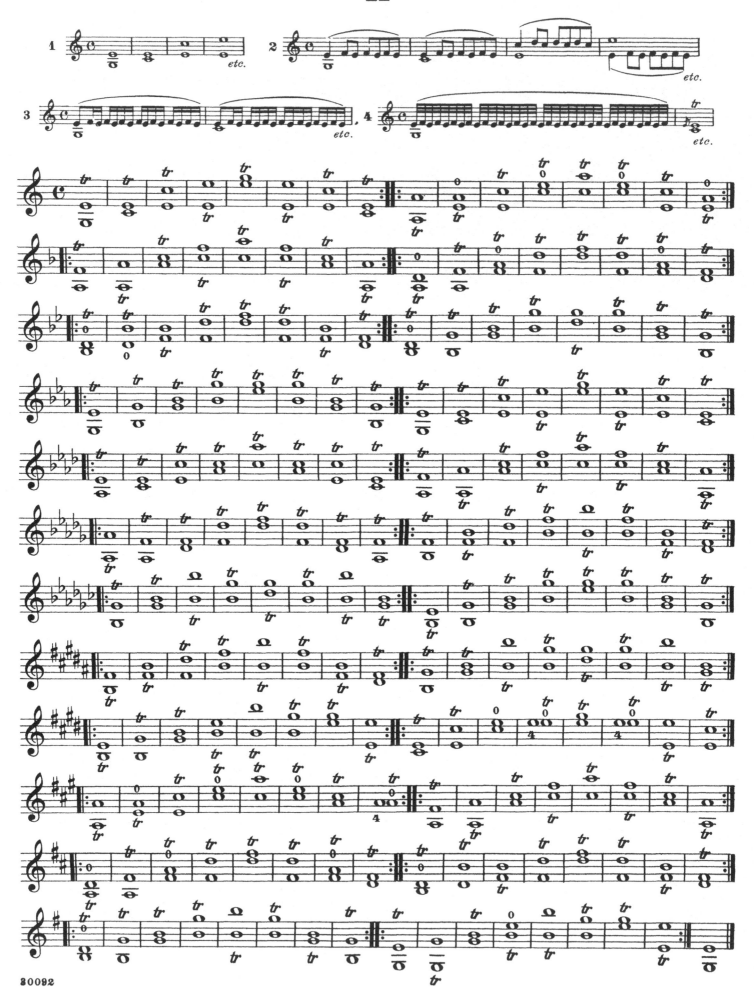

23